THE POCKET MENTOR:
INSIDER TIPS FROM AMERICA'S MOST SUCCESSFUL PEOPLE

BY

VINCE REARDON

CRYSTAL POINTE MEDIA, INC.
SAN DIEGO, CA

The Pocket Mentor: Insider Tips from America's
Most Successful People

By Vince Reardon

Cover Design by Laura Lehman

Copyright © 2015

Published April 2015

Published by Crystal Pointe Media, Inc.
San Diego, California

ISBN-13: 978-0692401507
ISBN-10: 0692401504

Testimonials

The Pocket Mentor is full of common sense lessons on life. Get it, read it, and pass it along to someone you love.

Ken Blanchard
Co-author of *The One Minute Manager®*
and *Refire! Don't Retire*

The Pocket Mentor is a treasure trove of ideas for how to live more authentic and fulfilling lives. Vince Reardon's selection of over 100 contributors is balanced and inspired, and includes some of the smartest, most interesting and successful people alive. The book contains the kind of hard-won wisdom that often comes too late in life. Recommended not only to those who will read the entries for themselves, but as a source of guiding principles and virtues for young people on the cusp of adulthood and the parents, mentors, and teachers who are guiding them.

Jean Rhodes
Professor of Psychology and Director of the
Center for Evidence-Based Mentoring,
University of Massachusetts Boston

Throughout history, mentoring has played a key role in passing on vital personal, cultural, and organizational knowledge in some form or another. Mr. Reardon has pulled together a terrific collection of advice here in one volume. Readers can learn and build on the collective wisdom of others to gain a head start on understanding many of life's most valuable lessons. We encourage readers to incorporate what they learn here into their personal lives as well as their professional lives for the benefit of society.

Vellore "Vetri" Vetrivelkumaran
CEO & Co-founder, Chronus Corporation –
Mentoring and Talent Development Software

Mentoring is such a critical tool in developing leadership potential and Vince Reardon has managed to assemble wisdom from over a hundred powerful mentors in a small, easy-to-read and digestible format that is full of thoughts for the reader to apply immediately.

Alison Martin-Books
Founder and CEO, Mentoring Women's Network

I wish to thank all my gracious contributors whose cooperation made this book possible.
All content was obtained from either phone interviews or email.

In loving memory of my dear friend and mentor
John Callahan

Table of Contents

Foreword

There are hundreds of paths up the mountain, all leading in the same direction, so it doesn't matter which path you take. The only one wasting time is the one who runs around and around the mountain, telling everyone else that their path is wrong.

Hindu Proverb

Preface

Let me be honest: when I was younger, I didn't take advice well. My mother never offered any and my father did nothing but tell me what to do. As I grew into manhood I didn't seek out advice, and if some well-meaning person offered it, I usually didn't listen. I learned to rely on my own counsel.

So here I am offering you advice—advice for finding your place in life—from 101 notable individuals. Why? When I look back on my life, I realize what a mistake I made. I should have listened more. I would have sidestepped more pitfalls and seized more opportunities.

It took years for me to turn this around. It took years to understand what the Greek philosopher Zeno meant when he said, "We have two ears and one mouth, so we should listen more than we say."

But you may wonder, "Can this advice really change my life?" Yes, it can. One piece of good advice can turn a life around. One piece of good advice can set a life on a never-dreamed-of course. The person one becomes and the path one pursues in life often pivot on a chance encounter, a fortuitous word, a gratuitous helping hand. As a character in a Philip Roth novel says, "It's so fickle, isn't it, who you wind up, how you wind up?"

Finally, the practical wisdom offered in this small book is time-tested and tear-stained. You can trust it; it has good bones. Some of it may be relevant now and some later. But don't just take my word for it. See for yourself.

On Finding Your Path

What path are you on? Where are you going in your life? These are questions I ask myself regularly. And they are questions you should ask too, if for no other reason than mild curiosity about your eventual destination. Yes, you will wind up somewhere.

Lewis Carroll famously said, "If you don't know where you're going, any road will get you there." But I don't believe you want to be on just *any* road. You want to be on the road that gets you to your destination as quickly and painlessly as possible.

As a college professor and mentor in a high school mentorship program, I speak with many young adults who don't know where they want to go, much less how to get there. I was no different at their age.

A part of the problem today is the disruption from the Great Recession of 2009. Many Americans, especially Millennials, who range in age from 18 to 33, feel disconnected from the traditional anchors of society—career, marriage, family, and religious and political affiliations.

Another part of the problem is their youth. Lacking experience and surrounded by myriad career choices, many Millennials lapse into a cocoon of indifference (*I don't have to decide yet*) or magical thinking (*I can do anything I want*) about the future.

Who can blame them? According to "Millennials in Adulthood," a 2014 study by the Pew Research Center, "Millennials are…the first in the modern era to have higher levels of student loan debt, poverty and unemployment, and lower levels of wealth and personal income than their two immediate predecessor generations (Gen Xers and Boomers) had at the same stage of their life cycles."

Still, I believe all people—young, middle-aged, and seniors—who have a direction and a destination achieve much more in life than those who don't. In the past five years, I've reached out to 101 high achievers—not celebrities, but men and women who have made a difference in the lives of others—and posed one question: *"What one piece of advice do you wish you had received when you were graduating from college or starting out in life?"*

The Pocket Mentor captures these invaluable tips and life lessons for you.

A word cloud analysis revealed that the five most common words in the book are: *life, people, learn, good,* and *think.* Interestingly, the four idols worshipped in our culture—money, fame, image, and consumption—appeared nowhere in the word cloud. However, five themes appear repeatedly in rich variety. They are: 1) be yourself, 2) be for others, 3) be a learner, 4) be persistent, and 5) be a risk-taker.

Be Yourself
Becoming yourself is a top priority of many *Pocket Mentor* contributors. Repeatedly, you are urged *not to fall in line, not to follow the crowd, not to settle for the fashion of the day.* Instead, you are counseled to become the person you were meant to be.

Be for Others
Love of neighbor, including the stranger, is the second most frequent theme in *The Pocket Mentor.* For many contributors, service to others is not optional; it is essential to living the good life.

Be a Learner
Lifetime learning is critical to *Pocket Mentor* contributors. If they aren't learning something new and sharing it with others,

life almost isn't worth living. Again and again you are encouraged to *leave your comfort zone, examine,* and *explore the world around you.*

Be Persistent

There's not one quitter in *The Pocket Mentor.* In fact, one might be tempted to say many are downright stubborn. But people who set big goals and achieve great things can be obstinate.

Be a Risk-Taker

Pocket Mentor contributors remind you that playing it safe doesn't get you very far. Still, many of us are paralyzed by the mere thought of taking a risk. The incomparable Peter Drucker said this about risk-taking: "People who don't take risks generally make about two big mistakes a year. People who do take risks generally make about two big mistakes a year." So why hesitate?

A word of caution: some tips overlap. A few could fit as comfortably in one category as another. For example, Dr. Redelmeier has ten tips. I placed his advice among the "Be a Learner" contributions because it seemed to capture the essence of his guidance, though it could have easily fit in another section.

Three final thoughts about *The Pocket Mentor:* first, the contributors aren't out-of-touch sages serving up spiritual comfort food. They are field-tested guides, mentors—Sherpas, if you will—who will help you find a path to the mountaintop. Second, each offers a word or two of advice, but you still must chop wood, haul water, and do the work. Third, despite their counsel, you will meet obstacles and fall on your face from time to time. This is a good sign. As Frank A. Clark once said, "If you find a path with no obstacles, it probably doesn't lead anywhere."

Enjoy the journey. It's the only way to appreciate the destination.

Be Yourself

David Agus, M.D.

Focus on what you're weak at, not on where you're strong. All too often we think, "I'm good at math. I'm going to do everything in math. I'm going to take math courses in college and I'm going to really excel there." But the people who succeed in life are the people who are well-rounded. So focus on what you're bad at and improve it.

When I was in training at Memorial Sloan-Kettering Cancer Center in New York, my team made a discovery that got a lot of attention. A Silicon Valley CEO came to me and said, "Agus, what you're doing is very interesting but you're not very good at describing it. You're not a good public speaker." I said, "I don't care. I'm a good scientist. That's what matters." The CEO said, "No, your job is also to educate and disseminate, to get the information out there. I'm going to help you schedule 100 lectures in six months at all of the local hospitals and schools." We did that, and I focused on improving what I was bad at, and it helped me for the rest of my life.

And that goes—not just for education—but for everything. For example, people who work out do the exercises they like and are good at. But they stay away from the ones they're bad at, and in the end that comes back to haunt them. It really is a powerful thing to know yourself and focus on what you're bad at.

Robert Ballard

You have to build confidence. Most important, you have to like yourself, not to be egoistic, but to come to grips with yourself. At some point in your career, generally I think when you are in your teens, you look in a mirror and you have to say, despite all the bumps and warts, "I like that person I'm looking at, and let's just do our best." It's at that point where you start to take what's good about you and polish it like an apple. Finally, be yourself. Then you are going to be really unique and exciting. People are going to beat a path to your door if you polish your inner self.

Benjamin Barber

Be true to yourself. People surrender the core of themselves for a job, success, or getting along with others. People don't hang on to what they believe.

David Bergman

I have learned no lessons from life, but I have developed some strategies for living, which I suppose amounts to the same thing. When I was coming out as a gay man in the early Seventies—a time when teachers were fired because they were gay rather than hired in Departments of Gender Studies—I had to decide whether to be open or discreet. I decided that it made no sense to try to hide the fact that I was gay, in part, because I wasn't a good actor, but mostly because it seemed a waste of time. Sooner or later one is discovered, and all the energy one spent hiding not only has gone for naught, but may also be used against one. I had grown up in the Fifties. My father, one of the gentlest, most moral men I have ever known, had been investigated by the FBI for his labor organizing, and I knew that if the State wanted to find out about my sexuality, it would. The strategy of not hiding my sexuality led to a strategy of living as openly as possible. Some people call me a jerk, but they can't say I've tried to hide my idiocy. Indeed, they may complain that I've flaunted it too frequently. Whether mine is a strategy that others should adopt, I can't say. It has not always made life easy, but it has made it simpler.

Nicole Boice

Personal
- Follow your passion and work with passion. People have made incredible careers doing what they love, and people get addicted to it and to you.
- Know that life is a journey, and you don't stop learning until you are in the grave.
- Listen, listen, and listen. Then speak.
- Ask questions.
- If you don't try, you will never know.
- Failure is not negative. It just gives you the information that you need to take another route. Try a different way; carve a different path.
- Don't take yourself too seriously. Laugh at yourself.
- Be honest, be transparent, and work with integrity.
- Be in the moment.
- Do or say something crazy and off the wall just to get people to laugh, smile, or roll their eyes.

Running a Business
- Follow your passion.
- Listen, learn, and then apply what suits you and your vision best.
- Hire people smarter than yourself.
- Celebrate every little milestone and appreciate the journey.
- Collaborate.
- Finally, work with a purpose.

William Bolcom

Do what you can't help doing. That's probably what happened to me. In the end, whatever choices I made, the good ones, have been the ones listening to my better nature. If you have something that goes against your better judgment, don't do it. The mistakes I've made in my life were done against my better judgments...A lot of people have it wrong. The idea is not to become famous. The idea is to do what you really want to do. And you may become famous from it or you may not, but at least you've done what you really wanted to do. Once you have that hunger [for fame], you're never satisfied. It's really hard to outgrow. I never particularly cared [for fame]. I just wanted to do what I wanted to do.

Scott Borg

There is something other people value that you can do better than other people. I mean this in a very practical, economic sense. You can do it better, because you can produce a better result at a lower cost. It might be something that your particular combination of abilities, skills, and experiences allows you to do extremely well. But it might be something you are unusually good at, not because your results are better, but because the cost to you is so low. It might be something that other people find a great deal of trouble, but you find hardly any trouble at all. I know there is something like this for you, because people are so extraordinarily different from each other. That difference is going to be your strength. So cherish that difference. Find the things your difference allows you to do better, more easily, perhaps more joyfully. Your special ability might simply be that you don't mind certain activities other people find a burden. Then, among the things you can do better than others, try to find the one that can deliver the most value to other people. That's the one where the difference between the cost to you and the benefits to others is greatest. When you've found that thing, look for a path in life where people will pay you for it. If you picked a path that really uses the things that make you different, you are going to be irreplaceable. And being irreplaceable is really nice.

Arthur Caplan

Listen carefully to advice from your mentors, family, and friends. Weigh it against your dreams, aspirations, and desires. Then, amalgamate both. If you are in any doubt or the advice is inconsistent, let your goals and values shape your choice. Pioneers need advice. Their problem is they can only get it from people who have not been there yet.

Sr. Joan Chittister, O.S.B.

I don't mean to be boring, but to thine own self be true. There is something about the process of life: finding out who you are, facing it, and allowing it to take you where you ought to be.

Dalton Conley

I think America has a strong, anti-intellectual tradition. It's not manly to do well in school. There's a strong sense of "You don't want to look or act engaged, like you're the teacher's pet, in school." And the reason I bring it up is I don't think it stops in school. It's in the boardroom too. I think in a lot of places people shy away from or have learned not to say the controversial thing. I don't mean the rude or inappropriate thing, necessarily, but the controversial thing, yes. And we're all the worse for it. I think if I gave one piece of advice, it would be to ask the inappropriate question. If you're afraid to ask that question, it's probably the right question to ask. Don't be afraid of offending somebody.

Lynne Cox

Go for your dreams. That's what keeps you alive and excited with your life. That's really it. There's nothing more exciting than following the path you were meant to follow and doing what you want to do. In the course of doing that, sometimes you aren't sure, but if you keep trying, you'll eventually figure out what it is you want to do.

Greg Evans

Everyone can leave some sort of legacy. Even if it's just to be remembered as a generous person or a good friend or a sympathetic listener. To leave a larger, more global legacy requires a unique ability or special characteristic that few people have. My advice, in this world of "You can be anything," is this: be realistic. Figure out what you can do and what you can't. Know your strengths and capitalize on them. Identify your unique qualities and put them to work for you. Those who leave a legacy are those who stand out from the crowd. Find a way to make yourself stand out, even just a little bit. Not everyone has the goods to be a superstar but everyone can find something in himself or herself that they can polish to a shine.

Gayle Lynn Falkenthal

Take advantage of being a beginner with a clean slate. You will only have one chance to start your career. Start it by putting a strong foundation under you. No one will expect you to know everything at first, and you shouldn't try to make anyone think that you do. Impress people not with your knowledge, but with your thirst for learning more. Ask every question possible. Later in your career, you might be afraid to seem foolish by asking a simple question. Listen far more than you talk. When you ask a question, stay quiet and really listen to the answer. People senior to you will be flattered and will share things it took them a long time to learn. You will gain mentors and admirers along the way simply by being open and receptive.

Mary C. Gentile

I used to worry about doing something that mattered, something that was worth doing. But I came to learn that if I did the things that were most engaging and compelling to me—the things that I most wanted and enjoyed doing anyway—then I was most likely making a positive impact in the world. That is, go with your own energy and passion rather than trying to force it into a mold that seems "most important" or "most needed" according to someone else.

David Lim

Don't sweat the small things, and appreciate the little things. Don't let too much get you excited. We all try living in the future. "I've got to make more money to do this or that," we say to ourselves. No! Try living more in the present and appreciate the things you have. You'll live a better life that way.

Kristin Neff, Ph.D.

The most important lesson I've learned is that we need to stop our endless quest for high self-esteem and instead learn how to be a good friend to ourselves in times of need. Self-esteem involves judging ourselves positively, but it is often contingent on being "special" and "above average." But we can't all be above average at the same time, and there is always someone doing it better. This means our self-esteem tends to bounce up and down according to our latest success or failure. Self-compassion does not involve judging or evaluating ourselves but is a way of relating to ourselves with caring concern. While we automatically extend our understanding and support to friends when they fail or make a mistake, we often beat ourselves up in the exact same circumstances. Self-compassion involves treating ourselves with kindness, remembering that all human beings are imperfect. Instead of feeling isolated by our struggles, we embrace ourselves as flawed works in progress, giving ourselves the emotional support needed to do our best. Research shows that self-compassion is a powerful form of emotional resilience, being linked to greater motivation and life satisfaction, less anxiety and depression, and more caring relationships. We can finally learn to be happy, therefore, not by stuffing ourselves into a box labeled *good*, but by being compassionate to ourselves when we need it most.

Eric Neudel

What I have learned is that we are very, very small, both in terms of size and in terms of time, especially time. I'm very interested in cosmology and the nature of the universe. When I look at the universe, I see we are smaller than tiny specks—smaller than the Higgs boson. We're also transient. That idea could lead us to despair, to nihilism, that our lives don't mean anything.

But, in fact, it's exactly the opposite for me. The lesson for me is that we, human beings, are generators of meaning. Generating meaning is everything. It's how we judge the nature of other people, and it's how we judge our lives.

I've always been a fan of Viktor Frankl. Like Frankl, I think we always have the ability, no matter what the circumstances, to interpret any situation the way we want to. No one can take that away from us. We can always resort to thinking of ourselves and others the way we want to think. We may not have the same values and assumptions as other people. But we don't have to be crushed by other people's opinions or other people's attitudes.

Because we are the generators of meaning, we can define ourselves all the time, every day. But we have to be true to ourselves. We have to be honest with ourselves and with everybody else. We should never lie, in any way. I know that seems dogmatic, but I have found that no matter what the situation is—even with security guards at borders—we can always tell the truth. The temptation is to lie about the most trivial things, but we don't have to. We never have to lie. And the most important thing is that we should never lie to ourselves. When we look at ourselves in the context of the universe and how massive it is, we have to rely on ourselves as the generator of our own meaning in life.

We shouldn't care what other people think of us. In life we'll go up and we'll go down. It's never clear how we will do in life. We're never great or nothing. Even the greatest person, the person with the greatest historical record, like a king or a queen, will fade in time. Ten billion years from now, there will be no trace of us. So what does that imply about our existence now? What does it infer? It infers we are here now; we have to generate our meaning; and we need to enjoy it. Yes, enjoy!

Christine Peterson

Save money until you can use it to buy freedom. I spent the first five years of my working career saving and haven't had to take a standard 9-to-5 job since.

Michael Shermer

The most important lesson life taught me is to not fool yourself, and you are the easiest person to fool. Thus we must always apply reason and science to everything we do. And to thine own self be true.

Bishop John Shelby Spong

We are to live fully; we are to love wastefully; and we are to be all that God intends us to be. That's because God is the source of life, God is the source of love, and God is the Ground of Being.

Eric J. Topol, M.D.

Think big and act bigger. There are no limits to what you can do if you have imagination without constraints. Each individual has unlimited potential. But it isn't just thinking about it, it's acting on it. Unfortunately, I didn't come to this realization until much later in life. I just wish someone had inspired me when I was young to think this way. I might have been more successful if I had an earlier start. I had to discover this on my own.

David Watson, Ph.D.

The lesson I learned that has shaped my career and life is not to worry too much about what others say or think about you and your life. I learned at an early age to do what you want to do. Pursue what you find interesting and worthwhile, and not what others think would be interesting and worthwhile for you. If you do what you—not others—find interesting, your life will be satisfying and fulfilling.

Be for Others

Monika Ardelt, Ph.D.

There is always more to learn, and I'm not talking about intellectual knowledge. There's always more to learn about yourself and your approach to life. That's what I think wisdom is—learning from experience and learning about yourself. There's a reason why we are here, and one of the reasons is learning certain lessons in life. And it never stops, unless you're the Buddha and have already reached enlightenment. But for us ordinary people there is always more. And sometimes learning these lessons is not always pleasant, but they are opportunities for learning more. When I was younger, I was hopeful that I'd get it, and sadly this is not how it works. There is always more.

The other thing I learned is that we are really social beings. We are not simply individuals; we are dependent on each other. And that has consequences. One of the things I've learned from my recent research—I looked at qualitative data from George Vaillant's Harvard Study, using my three-dimensional model of wisdom—was that men who really scored high [in the Study] cared about others. They showed a lot of giving, volunteering, working with others, and being part of the community.

What was really surprising to me was that those who scored consistently low always want more in life. They are never satisfied. Objectively speaking, these men are well off. They have good jobs, but they are self-centered. As a result, they are never happy, never satisfied. From a material point of view, their lives are pretty good. What I learned from this research is that self-centeredness is punished by feelings of dissatisfaction.

But if they're giving and have transcended their self-centeredness, they feel satisfied, no matter what the circumstances, even in old age when they don't have the best anymore. They're still showing contentment. This is not anything new. The research is trying to understand what has already been known. Jesus said, "Love your neighbor as yourself." We all hear it and think we understand it, but what does it mean?

What I've learned is that there are always deeper levels of understanding. I think that's one of them—being connected. We are social beings. If we try to exempt ourselves from that by living an individualistic life, it doesn't seem to go very well. It's a paradox. By giving of yourself and what you have, you find fulfillment. And by wanting more for yourself, you become diminished.

You cannot find fulfillment and satisfaction through egotistical means. It's all so fleeting. All the people who do the research in this area say, "This is not the way to go." All through the ages people have been saying this. No one has said, "If you really want to be happy, make a million dollars." That's not how it works.

Justin Brooks

The one piece of advice I wish I'd received when graduating high school was to only pursue a profession that I'd be passionate about. I was a business major in college because it was a safe path to a decent-paying job, but I was bored to death. Then I went to law school to become a corporate lawyer, something that also bored me. Fortunately, I got a job in law school working for a legal services office representing poor people. I realized I wanted a job where I could help the powerless. For the past 25 years, I've worked to free innocent people from prison. Giving hope to the hopeless and freedom to the wrongfully incarcerated have been my passion, my mission, and my life's work. If you can find that in life, you never feel like you are working.

Walter Brueggemann

Gifts are more important than achievements and possessions. That's because we live in a society of achievements and possessions, and it turns out we can't live by them. The older I get, the more I'm aware that the receiving and the giving of gifts really amount to the most. I would start with the gift of life, which is a gift from God and the continual giving of the gift of life by God. But then, [gift-giving] is mediated through us by our mothers, family, good neighbors, and good civic systems, such as education, medicine, and libraries.

Jerry Coleman

There are only two things in life worthwhile: those you love and who love you and your country.

Richard Cook

It means a lot more in context than just the words: "Let your conscience be your guide." It sounds sort of like a Jiminy Cricket thing [the fictional Disney character in the film *Pinocchio*]. It's simple but it means so much, and I truly believe it.

Nonie Darwish

I believe the most important attitude that will give you a satisfying life is selflessness, a giving attitude, and an attitude that every person on Earth is really a valuable person. I always look at the glass as being half full, not half empty, and treat people as if they're valuable. An attitude of gratitude is also important. When I came to America, I made friends very quickly. I'm so thankful. Some said, "Oh, you were discriminated against in America." I felt the exact opposite. I felt people were very gracious with me. I am very grateful to this country. I never lost the sense of being grateful.

Rev. Thomas Doyle, O.P.

The most important thing for me is finding serenity in life and living as much as humanly possible according to a code of integrity and decency. I've learned that self-absorption and narcissism are a very toxic weight. Those have been the primary causes of damage done to hundreds and hundreds of thousands of children, young people, and their parents from sexual abuse by Catholic priests.

Daniel Ellsberg

Don't do what I did. Don't wait until a war has started, for bombs to have fallen, until a thousand more people have died. If you have information that would give the lie to efforts to get us into a wrongful war, do what I wish I had done: go to the press and the Congress in order to put out the truth and save countless lives.

Kenneth W. Ford

Integrity is the most precious of all one's possessions. All of us cut corners sometimes. All of us tell white lies now and then. Yet without a core commitment to integrity, life is hollow, happiness is illusory, and civilization is impossible. Integrity is a requirement for meaningful human relationships, and likewise essential for research or writing or achievement of any kind. At bottom, integrity is necessary to one's sense of self-worth and one's sense that life is rewarding. I reached these conclusions as a teenager, when I first tried to think about the conditions for happiness and the conditions that make society work. Life since then has served only to strengthen them.

Annie Griffiths

The most helpful thing I learned was "Never operate from fear." The other is "The most satisfying act is when you're confident enough to give back to the world." It is really easy to forget that the world is filled with cultures that want peace, dignity, children, safety, etc. Africa is perhaps the most hopeful place.

Victoria Hale

You should figure out what your talents are, your gifts, and make the most of them. Don't hold back. Take them as far as you can. We're all on this planet for a reason; the world needs every person. The ultimate [reward] is serving others. Leave your comfort zone, go to parts of the world that frighten you. Stay there until you're not frightened. And when you have the opportunity, give. Then learn from others when they teach you something, and really, really take it in. The gifts flow in both directions.

Victor Davis Hanson

Develop a moral and spiritual code and do not allow events of the day—both spectacular victories and utter defeats— to change it. While it is easy to be introspective and self-critical amid disappointments, it is far more difficult, and far more critical, to remain unaffected by successes, and to remember that most are transitory—and have a far greater likelihood to lead to moral lapses than do trying times.

Lynn Harrell

Give back to your parents, your mentors, and your teachers. And make it easier for your fellow man. It can be as simple as taking a little extra time helping an old person cross the street rather than going your own way. One should base one's life on that humanitarian aspect. We all can say, "I should have given more money to the cancer drive or more money to support the hungry children you see on TV." But it starts in the environment in which we are living. Helping the cleaning lady who comes in. Giving an extra big tip to the sanitation worker whose son, you've learned, was killed in a gang war. It's reaching out to those around you.

Frances Hesselbein

Find a way to serve. Find a way to make a difference, however small. Whatever our work is, we always have time to serve, to volunteer, to make a difference in people's lives. I guess the bottom line is changing lives. When I speak to students on college and university campuses, I say, "To serve is to live." They applaud. This generation understands this.

Jeremy Hollinger

Listen well to others and yourself. Judge others and yourself gently, and double that compassion when you're tired or angry. Live the life you want now, and passionately. Keep even a broken heart open. Love unconditionally.

Gloria Killian

Look beyond yourself and see where there might be a real need. Don't be put off by dealing with people from a different world, especially prisoners and the homeless.

Ted Kooser

I was employed by a life insurance company for many years, and in the 1990s wrote a novel about a company convention in the Virgin Islands. I made fun of the foolishness of the salespeople as well as the home office staff who accompanied them. It was a sort of *Animal House* of the insurance business. I showed a section of the manuscript to a friend, Robert Knoll, an emeritus professor of English at the University of Nebraska, and he read what I showed him and laughed heartily at the funny moments, and then turned to me and said, "Ted, don't be too hard on those people. Nearly everyone is doing the best they can." I was then almost fifty years old, and it had never occurred to me that this was possible, or true, but over the years I've come to agree with my late friend. There are very few truly evil people in the world, and nearly everybody else is doing the best they can, often against terrible odds. I am very grateful for Robert's wisdom. The novel has never been published, and I am grateful for that, too. I would have regretted it.

Peter Korn

From my point of view, the question is not so much what piece of advice I wish I'd received, as what piece of advice I wish I'd truly heard. Every possible bit of life wisdom seems to have been in steady circulation for centuries, if not millennia. Early on, influenced by boyhood books and the 1960's counterculture, I bought into the admonition to march to one's own drummer. From Quaker education, I internalized the importance of finding a way to live that was spiritually rich, whether or not it was lucrative. What I wish I had also "heard" was just how psychically intertwined each of us is with the rest of humanity. We make our own happiness, yes, but there is scant joy to be found in isolation. To the extent that I have experienced the meaning and fulfillment that I equate with a good life, they exist in the difficult, sustained work of bringing something new into being that may prove of value to others as well as to myself.

Eugene Kranz

Think about the people who have been influential in your life, and take time out to say thank you to them. Then, very confidently, move forward in your life.

David Krieger

As a young man, faced with the Vietnam War, I learned to follow my conscience, rather than the path of least resistance. I learned that the U.S. government, or any government, can lie a country into war, but that it cannot prosecute that war without willing soldiers and a willing populace. I learned that a government can order a young person to kill on its behalf, but it can't force a young person to do so. I learned that a single committed person, young or old, can stand against the U.S. government and prevail. I learned that war is a terrible and often senseless tragedy, and that there are no good wars. I learned that wars are a foolish way to settle conflicts, and that nuclear weapons have made the potential destruction of war far more devastating. I learned that peace is not the space between wars, but rather a dynamic social process in which change occurs nonviolently. I learned that peace is not only an end but a means. I learned that peace requires perseverance, as does any great goal worth struggling for. I learned that we are all connected, with each other, with the past, and with the future. I learned that each of us has a responsibility to act for the common good and for generations yet to come, and that none of us has a right to give up on achieving a more peaceful and decent world.

Larry McReynolds

I'll be 55 years old [in January 2014]. I've been in NASCAR for well over 30 years—18 years as a crew chief and going on 13 years as a broadcaster. There are several things I've tried to take away from what I've learned and experiences I've had, and things I've tried to instill in my three kids, two of whom are adults now. The three things I've worked on throughout my life and career are: First, I've never asked anybody to do anything I won't do myself. When I was a crew chief, I would never ask a guy to stay later than I was willing to stay, or come in earlier than I was willing to come in, or ask him to ride in the van while I was riding in a plane. No matter what my title was or what another guy's title was, or if I was a crew chief and he was a painter, in God's eyes he's the same as I am.

Second, the biggest thing I probably preach—and I think it may be the one reason why I may have had success as a crew chief—is there is absolutely no substitute for good communication, whether on the personal or professional side. I'm a firm believer that failure in a business relationship, in a personal relationship between a husband and wife, a parent and child, or a brother and sister, is due to the lack of communication. I work very hard at communication in my job, in my business life, and especially in my personal life. I think that's why my wife and I have celebrated 30 years of marriage. We work hard at communicating with each other.

Third, I've always been proud of what I've accomplished—and I think it's what's made Chad Knaus and Jimmie Johnson so successful—but I've never sat still on those accomplishments. For example, today as a broadcaster I want to do a show that's better than the last show I did, even if I don't have any bad feelings about that last show. I still want to do a better job

53

with the next show. I took a page out of Nelson Stewart's book. He said he never pushed [his son] Tony to be the best race car driver that there was or is, but to be the best racecar driver than he could be.

Arnold Palmer

One word of advice that my father gave me that I have always passed along to others: "Always treat others the way you would like to be treated."

Sr. Helen Prejean, C.S.J.

We are all worth more than the worst thing we've ever done.

Erica Ollmann Saphire, Ph.D.

This is what I wish I had heard: Don't worry so much. When you do the right thing, and you do it well, you'll garner support. This is the best advice I can give: learn to communicate. Different kinds of people need information presented in different ways. Understand your audience.

Vin Scully

The most important lesson I have learned is to live by the Ten Commandments.

Barbara Van Dahlen

First, in general, people want to do good; they want to be good; and they want to help their fellow man. But for most people, that's not an easy thing to figure out how to do. If we don't help them, if we don't provide opportunities, if we don't create vehicles, and if we don't channel that good, we've lost tremendous potential to do good in the world.

Second, this kind of work, whatever we want to call it—doing good in the world, addressing needs in our society or in the global community—is really hard work. I would read about people like Mother Teresa, or Martin Luther King, Jr., or Gandhi, and I'd think, "Oh my God, what they're doing is so hard. Why are they doing this? What keeps them doing this?" Over the last seven years, the one thing I've learned is that it's incredibly difficult, but it's also the most amazing gift to be able to help others. I'm incredibly blessed to have the opportunity do this kind of work.

Third, the only way we can solve the real issues in our world is if we coordinate efforts and if we collaborate. And again, that sounds simple too. But I have learned that it's extremely difficult to do—to effect change by encouraging folks to collaborate and coordinate. It's very difficult to ask people to park their agendas at the door and to think of the big mission, to think of the big needs. But if we're effective, if we're able to do that, great things will happen.

Ricardo "Cobe" Williams

If you have a child, be a parent. One of the things that could have made a big difference was having my father in my life. As a kid I grew up in a household around people selling drugs, hustling all their life—a big brother, cousins, and my father. My father was my role model, so I wanted to be like him. He was selling drugs; he had slick cars, jewelry, and flashy stuff. When I was six or seven years old, my father went to prison. When he got out of prison—I was 11 years old—he was killed. Growing up in the community [Englewood, on the South Side of Chicago] I wished I had my father. The people I was running around with all had one thing in common—we didn't have a father in our life.

Spending quality time with a kid is so important. I remember when I was little my father used to take me to baseball and basketball games. He liked sports. I remember sitting with him and watching the games. Spending that quality time with him showed me something else—something other than the drug life. Quality time spent with a parent means everything to a little kid. Today, I am a father figure, an uncle figure, and a brother figure to kids. I meet these kids where they are; I don't judge them. I understand these kids. I understand that they make bad choices. They act out many times because they're looking for attention. They need guidance. So not having a father, a man in their life, is hard for them. I just want to be there for them—in the way I wish my father had been there for me.

Be a Learner

Daniel Callahan

One thing I've found valuable in my life is to read very widely, and read both sides of an issue. Get a good sense of how people think. And keep your eyes open. I became interested in medical issues and [founding] the Hastings Center because these [biomedical] issues kept popping up all over the place, in magazines for instance.

George Church, Ph.D.

Distrust aphorisms. It is far better to harness complexity and diversity than to search for falsely comforting simplicity. Even physics, which gave us some of the pithiest of our predictive statements of truth, is increasingly embracing complex systems. In biology and engineering, complexity certainly has enormously positive consequences—albeit requiring considerable trial-and-error evolution. The key partner of complexity is diversity of the systems under selection and diversity of the selective forces themselves. Conventional engineering is typically focused on one key product or prototype, while bioengineering can look at trillions of prototypes at once. Life is literally giving engineers important lessons on diversity and selection.

Marva Collins

Perhaps the most important thing you can do is to set a good example by making sure your children see you read often. In addition, read something to your children every day, no matter how old they are. Even adolescents need and often want you to read to them, or to have them read to you. Reading to or with them is a good way to discover their strengths and weaknesses. Follow the reading sessions with questions, such as, "What happened in that story? What do you think will happen next?"

Temple Grandin

One thing I figured out very early on was seeing doors to opportunity. Many years ago, early in my career, I got the business card of the editor of the *Arizona Farmer Ranchman* magazine, who I later approached about doing an article. I wrote the article for the magazine, and before long I had a press pass from the magazine, which got me into cattle meetings. So if you meet the right person, he or she can open the right door for you.

A lot of young people today don't figure that out. If you want to get into a job, walk up to the guy who has the tech company ID badge around his neck and show him your work. If you're a writer or an artist, you need to show off your portfolio. People thought I was a weird geek. No one wanted to talk to me. Then I'd show them my drawings [of signs and corrals for cattle ranches] and they'd say, "Ooh, you did that!" Then I started getting a little bit of respect. When I meet parents who tell me that their kids are really good artists, I tell them, "Well, get your kid's art on your phone. You never know when you might meet someone who can open a backdoor." But a lot of people today tell me, "I never thought of that." I'm very good at finding backdoors.

A lot of kids don't know where they're going. I gave a guest lecture to an environmental management class at a university in 2013 and they gave me their questions on index cards. The big question was: "How did you get your passion for cattle?" I said I was exposed to them when I was a teenager. Kids are not going to get interested in things they aren't exposed to. Schools have taken out hands-on classes. How are you going to find out if you like a musical instrument if you've never used one? If I hadn't had art when I was in school, I would have gone nowhere. I had a wakeup call during this class [in environmental management] I was teaching. Here are regular students saying, "I don't really know what I want to do." I always tell students, "Before you go into an advanced degree, try on a career first. Make sure it's what you want to do." Many students today are not doing enough things to find out what they would like to do.

People have a real bad way of staying in their silos. One thing I've tried to do is get out and look at the neuroscience of cattle behavior and get involved in how to build stuff. Both construction and neuroscience are used in my work now, although they sound like totally different things. I follow employment trends. Employers in the tech industry don't want a pure electrical engineer or a pure computer science major. They want computer science, a little electrical engineering, and throw a little mechanical engineering in there too. They like these mixtures. What I've done my whole life in my career is mix up construction work with neuroscience and animal science. But it all relates, and I use it all to work on the things I work on. Most people stay in their silos, and it's hard to bust out of silos.

Erin Gruwell

As an English teacher, I am fond of metaphors. The most important lesson I learned as a teacher was that it was more important for me to be a student. I walked into a classroom with 150 kids under the guise or the ruse that I was going to be a teacher and give them wonderful life lessons. But the most important thing I learned when I walked out of Room 203 all of those years later was that I had 150 teachers who taught me valuable lessons. And it wasn't about literature. Essentially, it was about Life 101.

I have always been a student, always a lifelong learner, and always receptive to learn lessons from others. In retrospect, I believe it's the Socratic method, which I didn't realize I was going to implement. A lot of teachers walk into a classroom and talk *at* kids or *to* them, and for me it was the wonderful, magical role reversal.
In the film *The Freedom Writers* [the actor playing] my dad said, "You are blessed with a burden." I think that says a lot—that duality—both as a teacher and a student. The more you learn, the more it is a burden. You are more cognizant of the world and your place in the world. That's a huge burden. What's important is what you do with that burden.

All these years later, those 150 kids are still very much a part of my life. We've taken our class's story and made it a much larger story. I'm still learning, I'm still being challenged, and I'm still asking questions. I'm still very much a student of life, and I love that.

Jim Hall

Allow yourself to grow every day, especially musically. You get so much back from music; it's so personal. It doesn't matter if you can make a living with it, although I'm fortunate I can.

Joy Harjo

I am constantly reeducating myself to be a real human being. A real human being knows that everything in this universe, even time, is a being. We "civilized" human beings are considered foolish, even lost by most of the others who share this realm with us. Most have lost the ability to communicate with the winds, trees, stones, birds, creatures, insects, the sea, or fire and stumble about in strange ambitions to own more or to be famous. These abilities of perception and communication live within us and are given to us to be useful. When I imagine myself the same size as the head robin who lives in my yard, when I stay still and listen, I can understand his perceptions. His world is just as large and dynamic as my own, with a similar dance of hungers and joys. The robin world is neither below nor above the human world, and so it is with all creatures. I have learned to step respectfully and carefully, in this diverse universe of human beings of all kinds, including robin.

Leroy Hood

In terms of career my advice is twofold: 1) do something fascinating and challenging, and 2) do something that's fun.

We have to spend our life excited every day.

Mari-Luci Jaramillo

Be prepared for the future. Get the best, broadest, and most basic education you can. If later you have to change careers, work on the specialty requirements. You can change careers often, with a minimum of effort, if you have a solid basic education.

Robert Kenner

I didn't graduate from college because I got right into the movie business. I can't say what I wished I had heard [in terms of advice from others], but I can say what was the best thing that happened to me. I had mentors, people who loved what they were doing. Their enthusiasm lit a fire under me, and I realized that that's what I wanted to do—make documentary movies. So I advise you to find people who are doing something in a field that you might want to go into, find people who are doing it well, and learn from them. That was the best thing that happened to me—to meet these wonderful mentors who lit a fire for me. Ironically, they're in their mid-70's and they're still teaching me. People like Don Lenzer, the cinematographer who shot *Woodstock* [the movie], and Nick Noxon, who ran *National Geographic*. They were wonderful teachers, and they encouraged me to do what I wanted to do.

I took a brief hiatus [from documentaries] when I got involved in theatrical, dramatic movies and I lost my center, my focus, when I tried to do that. I was always trying to guess what other people wanted. But when I was making documentaries, I got to do what I found interesting and follow my own path. It's much more exciting when you're connected to your own inner core than trying to guess what other people want you to do.

Stephen M. Kosslyn

It's not about being good or bad at something; it's about fit. You shouldn't evaluate yourself based on your successes or failures, but instead you should try to learn from them about your fit with certain tasks, situations, and contexts. Be modest in your successes, and give yourself a break in your failures. But be attentive, and learn how better to select your challenges for the future.

Alan Lightman

I have learned several important lessons in my life.

(1) Everything is impermanent. The nature of existence is change. We often get so hung up trying to repeat an experience or a state of mind in the past that we are unable to live in the present, or proceed to the future. But nothing stays the same in life. Everything comes and eventually passes away. That is the natural way of life and of the universe as a whole.

(2) The greatest joy in life comes from helping others. We are frequently fixated on our own pleasures, but the deepest pleasure comes from giving to other people.

(3) Rewards in life are often not handed out according to merit. Luck and chance play a significant role in the outcome of events. The sooner we learn this lesson, the happier we will be. Instead of continually beating ourselves up because we do not receive the recognition or fame or fortune we think we deserve, we should recognize that life is not necessarily "fair." All we can do is the best we can do with each enterprise, try our best, and the rest is beyond our control.

(4) Much of our stress, unhappiness, and disappointment originates within our own minds and is tangled up with our own egos, rather than being an intrinsic part of external events.

74

Tom Morris

The single most important thing I've learned as a philosopher is that life is supposed to be a series of adventures, lived with love, confidence, and a real concern for others, as well as ourselves. The adventure we're on right now, whatever it might be, is preparing us for the next one, and often in ways we can't even imagine. The uncertainty of the future is just the open field for adventure and creativity that we all need, moving forward, even though it can feel uncomfortable at times. The key to successful living is to be open to new ideas and new possibilities along the way. Your ongoing job is, then, what I call "3-D Living"—Discover your talents, Develop those talents, and Deploy them into the world for the good of others, as well as yourself. This is a threefold task that never ends.

Michael Nagler

The most important lesson I have learned—and I'm still working on it—is that through meditation we can take our evolution into our own hands. We are not limited to the senses and the intellect but can gradually become directly aware of reality when we learn to bring the mind gradually under our own control—that is, the control of our better judgment and higher instincts. If we're following a genuine method of meditation, one that slows down and focuses the mind, usually under the guidance of a good teacher, even a little progress brings us a sense of security we've always sought, along with happiness that doesn't dissipate with the passage of time, more rewarding relationships, and better health. It allows us to find our purpose in life and pursue it.

Carol North, M.D.

My advice to myself is "Apply yourself." If there's a problem, apply yourself, and work at a solution. If there's not an easy solution, work hard and make it happen. It's pretty basic, but that's the thing that I've always relied on and it's always come through for me.

Mark Potok

I think the most important piece of advice one can give a young person in life is "Be curious." If you are curious, the world is open to you. If you are curious, there's always a reason to keep on living, to keep on fighting for good things, and to keep on learning. Without curiosity in this world, you're lost. There are no reasons to stick it out. That to me is the key to living a good life—curiosity.

Donald A. Redelmeier, M.D.

- The capacity to change your mind is the best evidence that you have one.
- Be familiar with the entire battlefield, including the element of surprise.
- Choose your battles and then fight for all you are worth.
- Digging for treasure is hard, yet not as hard as proving there is no buried treasure.
- Success will test your mettle more than any single failure.
- The dream of success means nothing without the will to prepare.
- Respect all hazards, for when you least respect them you will least expect them.
- Respect all that might come to replace you; if not, they will do so more quickly.
- Reveal only that which returns to assist your cause.
- Laugh at yourself more than at arrogant souls who take themselves too seriously.

Roger Rosenblatt

Wait. I don't know if waiting on one's actions or reactions is the most important of life's lessons, but it certainly is useful. Wait before anger. Wait before judgment, or excessive enthusiasm or even compassion. The mind at its best is a slow animal. It contains too much information and experience to be rushed into answers. Wait, and let the answers come to it.

Douglas Rushkoff

I don't really have a single life lesson. In some ways, I guess my life lesson has been not to look for a single life lesson. I've stopped looking for the big answer, the ultimate truth, the moment of awakening. There is none. That's the whole point. As Westerners, we got quite obsessed with the Aristotelian narrative: hero's journey, climbing up the path until climax. And with that climax comes the Great Recognition, the Moment of Truth. Well, reality just isn't like that. There are lots of truths, and lots of moments. We end up missing most of them if we keep our eyes on the prize.

So giving up on that, accepting incremental change and learning as the real path toward any sort of progress, is both liberating and sobering. It means we just have to keep walking, keep our eyes open, and accept that those wonderful flashes are usually just fireworks.

Jeffrey Wigand

Read Aristotle, Plato, Mill, Rawls, and Putnam. I wasn't exposed to them in school, and I went through a lot of school. Aristotle has lots of things to say that are important today. One widely accepted idea in our culture is that the good life consists in accumulating pleasure and avoiding pain. But Aristotle taught that man derives intrinsic happiness not from maximizing pleasures or minimizing pain but through virtuous action. That's a 2,300-year-old idea that is applicable today.

Be Persistent

Dave Brubeck

No matter what happens, try to move forward.

Albert G. Crenshaw, Ph.D.

Growing up in the 1960s and 1970s, and having a less-than-privileged background, I was encouraged by those around me to go to college. The premier goal was to get that degree, no matter what the topic was. Actually having the degree was not really the ultimate goal, but it was obviously a door-opening tool. At this stage of my life or even a little earlier (my sophomore or junior year at university) I wish I had been pressed to open discussion about *where I wanted to go in life* and *what I wanted to work with*. I wish that I had been advised to look at my long-term goal and then encouraged to work backwards to realize how to reach it. Instead, I stood there with my degree and asked myself, What can I do with this? Ultimately, I let doors open for me, instead of knocking on the door that I eventually chose. Fortunately, I ended up in an area—research scientist—that I probably would have chosen anyway, but it took time and a bit of luck. Whereas, if I had known about this profession early on, I would have arrived here much sooner and perhaps had more time to contribute—and much more fun. So, my advice is to decide where you want to go early in life, work backwards to realize your ambition, and let nothing limit your dream.

William Michael Dillon

- Never give up on yourself, even if others do.
- When you think you are in the worst possible situation, just look around, and put it in perspective. You will see many people who are suffering more than you are.
- Always stay true to yourself when others want to change you.
- When people hurt you, generally they will apologize. But when people do bad things intentionally, they will do their best to cover it up.
- Always get an attorney whether you are innocent or guilty.

Anne Kelly Knowles

Follow your heart and put up with the heartache. Throughout my life, including my academic career, I have fallen passionately in love with various pursuits and each one of them has posed unanticipated difficulties, which at times have been heartbreaking. But what I have found over the decades is that the joy that comes from doing what I love more than makes up for the difficult times.

One example would be falling in love with the discipline of geography, which explained the world to me. It made sense of everything. I discovered geography late in my twenties. I went to graduate school at 30 to study geography. I got my master's [degree] and Ph.D., and then discovered that employment was declining in my discipline. My particular passion was historical geography and nobody was hiring, and I mean nobody in the United States. So I took a job in Wales, but that was not the place I wanted to live long-term. When I looked back at the United States, again no departments were hiring in historical geography. I applied for 60 jobs in the United States before I finally got a few interviews at places I would want to live. The only job offer I got was at Middlebury College [in Vermont], which is where I am today.

I'm not a fatalist, but I don't believe that things always turn out for the best. I was being really stubborn and insisting on being an historical geographer when that was hopeless. But I couldn't help it because that was what I loved. After 20 years of sticking it out, what I have been doing all along turned out to be something people are now interested in. And you never know if that's going to happen. It might not have happened for me. It has, and that makes me that incredibly happy. It's funny how fashion goes in the world of ideas. It's governed by fashion as much as fashion is.

Mel Leipzig

Stick to your guns. Everybody has his or her soul, especially if you're an artist. You almost instinctively know, if you're an artist, what you want to do. You should not allow yourself to be swayed by fashion or teachers or even your parents. You know who you are and stick to yourself. I am what one critic called "a rock-ribbed realist." I studied [at Yale University and Cooper Union in the 1950s] with all abstract painters, and if I had listened to what they wanted me to do—abstract expressionism or color concepts by Josef Albers—I would be nowhere now. Nowhere. Stick to your guns!

Phillip Lopate

The most important lesson life taught me was not to kill myself. I learned it by trying unsuccessfully, when I was a college sophomore, to do myself in. Afterwards, I abjured not only self-destruction, but extremes of all kinds, including yearnings for total happiness, spiritual transcendence, psychic merger with another, and apocalypse. I pursued the "middle way," with a large dose of stoicism and, whenever possible, corrective humor. I learned not to take myself so seriously. If that restraint meant the continual exercise of skepticism and irony (which some regard as soul-corroding), *tant pis (French: "Too bad." Literally, "So much the worse")*. My goal remains to get through life without killing myself, and in that regard, I have so far been a smashing success.

Alfred Lubrano

Never blow your *sprezzatura*. It's a term from the Italian Renaissance, from *The Book of the Courtier* by Baldassare Castiglione. It means an easy nonchalance. Never let them see you sweat. When I got my first newspaper job in Columbus, [Ohio], I was given an assignment to cover an RV show. Growing up in Brooklyn, I didn't know what an RV [recreational vehicle] was. Does it mean "random violence"? I didn't know, but I sure wasn't going to ask my editor. Don't let them see you sweat. *Sprezzatura!*

Robert J. Maurer, Ph.D.

One [life lesson], which has prompted me to write the books I've written, is the power of taking very small, incremental steps when there's some task that I'm very much committed to but overwhelmed by. Like most people, I tend to make changes only in the face of some overwhelming evidence. When things aren't working out, I desperately want the steps to come very quickly. So, taking very small steps in the face of hunger and desire for large change is one lesson I've learned in my life.

Next, having been raised to be very self-reliant and independent, I had to learn to allow myself to reach for emotional and technical support. That's so crucial to success in any endeavor. It's one I'm still learning because it's not easy to ask for help sometimes.

There is a saying in Zen that you only teach what you need to learn. And I'm afraid I'm guilty of that because these lessons have been so important to me. I've spent a lot of time researching and teaching them. And in teaching them, I would hope to reinforce my own willingness to follow the precepts of taking small, incremental steps and reaching for emotional and technical support.

John McKnight

A professor at Northwestern University, Irving Lee, taught me a lesson in leading an effective life. He said you should have reduced expectations and increased motivations, and if you get it the other way around, your life will be ineffective.

Frank Meeink

I tell the kids I coach, probably within the first couple of days that I meet them, "I don't count how many times you fall down. I only count how many times you get back up." I tell them, "Later in life, that will always stick with you. No matter what you fail in, no matter how far you fall, whatever your trials and tribulations, if you get back up, then you're never beaten. The other team may win the game, but they never beat you personally, as long as you get back up and play the game."

In my life, there were times when I had just about given up. And when I look back on those times, I did get back up. I have always tried to make the best of it. When I finally gave up on the neo-Nazi movement, I was 19 years old and I knew for the longest time that I had been on the wrong team. So it was time to give up. At the time, it was everything that I had. I had distanced myself from my family; my family had distanced itself from me. So all I had was this movement. I gave everything to it because that's how I do it in life—I gave it *everything*! And I finally had to start admitting that this was wrong.

I became the racist that everyone knows in their life: the racist that makes exceptions all the time. You know, "I hate all black people, except John. John's cool, he's a nice guy." Or, "I hate all black people except Rodney. Rodney's cool, I went to school with him." I hated *that* [excuse] more than I hated other people. I hated that I was always making exceptions but I was still an idiot for being a racist. Today, my whole message is empathy. Everything I do—speaking, lecturing, and writing—is all about empathy.

Danny Rubin

The truth is there is nothing I could say to myself now that I didn't already know then [in young adulthood]. Don't get me wrong—that first year after college, for example, was easily the toughest, most anxious, frightening, and uncertain of any year of my life before or since. But there is still nothing I can think of that I could say to that poor kid! For one thing, I don't look at my past choices as having been wrong or right, and so there are no mistakes to redress. I couldn't even have told him to lighten up and trust his future because he already knew that—and it was still difficult. I may be saying that I am no wiser now than I was then. I may also be saying that plotting my path, making my choices, taking my lumps, wrestling with uncertainty, and formulating my values through these life experiences has always been, for me, the point. And it leaves me with nothing to say to my young adult self, except, "Keep going. You're going to like it."

Mubin Shaikh

Know that this is only the very beginning. Many hills and valleys shall appear without you knowing what lies on the other side. When you reach them, take a break, hydrate, and just keep moving.

Dennis Smith

Ask any of my kids and they'll tell you I tell them this all the time—"Keep the wagons moving." The idea is that it's very easy to get depressed and feel stuck and think your life is unimportant. But I would refer you to St. Francis of Assisi, who never felt his life was unimportant. Even in the early days, after he left his family, when he was in extraordinary impoverishment, he always knew his life was God's gift. Consequently, you should never feel morose about not doing what you should have done. You should feel that where you are today is as good as you could make it. And if you keep the wagons moving, you can make it better.

Frank Sulloway

Everyone has to find his or her own formula for success and fulfillment in life. We know this from evolutionary biology as well as psychology. The secret to success is finding and maximally exploiting your own niche...My overall advice to others would be to find something that you are both good at and really love doing. Then, try to find a way to earn a living doing what you love. With persistence, more things are possible than one might think, but not more than one might dream.

Stuart W. Thorn

A sailboat, powered only by the wind, can reach its destination even in the face of a howling gale blowing directly against it, just by zigzagging a bit. So can you. A bat may be blind, but she still finds her way by listening to the echo of her own inner voice and distinguishing it from all the others. So can you.

Harry Wu

Keep yourself in freedom. I didn't have my freedom for so many years. When I passed through [U.S.] Customs [from China] and was finally free, I knelt down on the floor and said to myself, "I'm free! I'm free!" To understand the preciousness of freedom you need to lose it for a couple of years. Then, and only then, will you begin to understand the treasure that is freedom.

Be a Risk-Taker

Stacy Allison

Find your passion, what drives you to do your best. You will
have a lot of failures and have to take a lot of risks, but as time
passes, it will make all the difference in the world.

Anthony Atala, M.D.

I wish I had been advised that while it's important to have goals and ambitions, it is equally important to be open to the unimagined possibilities that life offers. I think it is important for young people starting out not to be so set on a particular path that they miss out on other opportunities. I had always been interested in a career as a physician, and had never even considered research. In fact, I had to be talked into doing a research fellowship after I finished my medical training. Yet once I started on that path, I realized I didn't want to turn back. Research has been an important part of my career and life ever since.

Jack Coleman

Go where your heart and your head tell you to go. Not someone else's heart and head—yours. The word that has played a very big part of my life, particularly since my blue-collar sabbaticals, is *dignity*. Dignity plus integrity spells goodness. One conclusion I came to a number of years ago is that when I die, if I had a tombstone, I would want it to read: "I'm glad I did rather than I wish I had."

Lois P. Frankel, Ph.D.

I wish someone had told me that our lives and careers are not linear. We are mistakenly led to believe that we have to know at age 21 what we will be doing at age 31, 41, and 51. The reality is, if you remain open to possibilities and continue to grow intellectually, personally, and spiritually, you can't possibly know where the path will take you. The important thing is to remain true to your values, put your given talents to good use, and not be afraid to take risks because Lao Tzu was right when he said, "Leap and the net will appear."

Rev. George Houser

I have always been fond of these lines of verse from Cardinal
John Henry Newman:

> *Lead, Kindly Light, amid the encircling gloom*
> *Lead Thou me on!*
> *The night is dark, and I am far from home—*
> *Lead Thou me on!*

Tom Kundig

As a kid, I was raised in a culture of apprenticeship, basic training, which was fundamentally important to me. In this culture, before you made the next move, there was a mentor, or a Buddha, teachers, the people you work with, and the people you worked alongside. They didn't have to be in a leadership position; they could be colleagues, people who might surprise you. In my case, I learned a lot working alongside other union laborers at construction sites or people who worked in sawmills. In some ways, I learned as much from them as I learned from my real mentor, who was an artist who taught me how to work hard, taught me how to think about life, and taught me how to think about moving materials, shaping materials, through an idea.

It all centered on the idea that you have to spend many years practicing before you can take a risk. For me, that's the most important life lesson. Taking risks is ultimately the most important thing, and it can take any form. It can take the form in the past experience of mountain climbing; it can take the form in the architecture I practice; it can take the form of relationships.

When I look back at my life, those moments that changed my life were the moments when I took a risk. But before you can take a risk, you need some basic training so you can take a thoughtful risk.

Robert Langer

The most important lesson I learned in my life—after having had many people tell me that many of my ideas and inventions would never work or never come to fruition—is that this is very rarely true. I think if you really believe in yourself, if you are persistent and work hard, there is very little that is truly impossible.

Daniel Levitin, Ph.D.

Be flexible. I planned to become an electric guitar player but was offered a position as a bass player in a band. The band did well, but instead of continuing as a bass player, I was offered a position as a producer and an arranger. I took that. That led to becoming a record company executive. I didn't plan any of these things. All I knew was that I wanted to be in the music-making business. I didn't end up doing what I originally wanted to do, but it was a great ride.

Nancy Lieberman

Be fearless. Have humility. And remember, never be afraid of failure. Failure is noble. It means you tried something outside your comfort zone.

Debra Liebert

Your life matters. Today's decisions and choices mold your tomorrow—make sure they reflect what is important to you and what you value. In the confusion of making decisions when consequences may be unknown, remain open to opportunity while taking a deep look at yourself. You are the steward of your tomorrow. This is your life, live it well!

Patricia Limerick

If there is some activity, project, or undertaking that makes you feel frightened and uncomfortable, then that's the thing you probably better do. And for various reasons, you might be very good at it, so what a shame it would be if you stayed out of it. If it turns out you don't have a talent there, just letting the dragon know that it has lost its power to scare you is good for you and good for the dragon.

Mario Livio

There is a lot to be said for following your dreams. But unfortunately dreams sometimes turn out to be just that—dreams. I, therefore, recommend a balanced approach. Do follow your dreams, but don't hesitate to ask for advice from the experienced, and try to shape your path so that it incorporates that advice. At the end, as Oscar Wilde once noted: "We are all in the gutter, but some of us are looking at the stars." Do your best to look at the stars, without forgetting that we may be in the gutter.

Michelle Mueller

I wish someone had told me that I'd make mistakes, lots of them! And that I'd learn from each and go forward with that knowledge to be better and make a difference. If you aren't making mistakes, you aren't taking enough risks or expanding your universe. Embrace your mistakes and realize they stretch you in ways you have never imagined. Take risks and reach for the stars now. This is not a practice life—this your real life!

Adam G. Riess

It's a cliché but true: do what you love and you will never work
a day in your life.
You will be happier doing what you love for half the money
than what you do not for twice.

Emily Warner

Ask your parents for a flying lesson or two for your birthday. Also, take aviation-related classes in school and participate in educational programs for young people at nearby aerospace museums.

Wendy Wong

Life is so short! Do all the things that matter to you, while you feel the tug to do them. Don't resist or put off those tugs. One adventure will lead to another.

Afterword

Pursue some path, however narrow and crooked, in which you can walk with love and reverence. Whenever a man separates from the multitude and goes his own way, there is a fork in the road, though the travelers along the highway see only a gap in the paling.

Henry David
Thoreau

Biographies

David Agus, M.D., is a physician and a *New York Times* bestselling author. He is a professor of Medicine and Engineering at the University of Southern California.

Stacy Allison was the first American woman to reach the summit of Mt. Everest in 1988. Stacy's experiences extend well beyond the mountains. She owns and operates Stacy Allison General Contracting. She and her team of builders specialize in high-end restoration. In the spirit of giving back to her community, Stacy chairs the American Lung Association of Oregon's largest fundraiser, *Reach the Summit.*

Monika Ardelt, Ph.D., is an associate professor at Florida State University. She studies wisdom and life satisfaction in old age, the development of wisdom throughout life, the relation between wisdom and spirituality, and aging and dying well.

Anthony Atala, M.D., is the director of the Wake Forest Institute for Regenerative Medicine and the W.H. Boyce Professor and Chair of the Department of Urology at Wake Forest University. Dr. Atala is a practicing surgeon and a researcher in the area of regenerative medicine. His current work focuses on growing new human cells, tissues, and organs.

Robert Ballard is a former U.S. Naval officer and professor of Oceanography at the University of Rhode Island. He is noted for his underwater archaeology, especially underwater shipwrecks, including his discovery of the *Titanic.*

Benjamin Barber is a senior research scholar at the Center on Philanthropy and Civil Society of the Graduate Center, the City University of New York, the president and founder of the Interdependence Movement, and Walt Whitman Professor of Political Science Emeritus, Rutgers University. He is the author of *Jihad vs. McWorld,* published in 1996, and *If Mayors Ruled the World,* published in 2013.

David Bergman is a poet and professor of English at Towson University in Towson, Maryland, which is part of the University System of Maryland. In 2000 he was presented with the Lambda Literary Award for Anthologies/Fiction.

Nicole Boice is the founder and president of the Global Genes Project, one of the leading rare and genetic disease patient advocacy organizations in the world. The organization unites experts, advocates, and patients to promote awareness and research into the 7,000 rare and genetic diseases affecting approximately 30 million Americans and more than 350 million people worldwide.

William Bolcom is a composer of chamber, operatic, vocal, choral, cabaret, ragtime, and symphonic music. He has received the Pulitzer Prize, the National Medal of Arts, and two Grammy Awards.

Scott Borg is the founder of the U.S. Cyber Consequences Unit, a research institute that provides assessments of the strategic and economic consequences of possible cyber-attacks and cyber-assisted physical attacks. Borg, who is considered one of the world's foremost experts in cyber security, has lectured at Harvard, Yale, Columbia, and other leading universities throughout the world.

Justin Brooks is a criminal defense attorney, a professor of law at California Western School of Law in San Diego, and the director and co-founder of the California Innocence Project

(CIP). CIP is dedicated to obtaining the release of wrongfully convicted inmates. In November 2014, Brooks and the CIP were instrumental in obtaining the exoneration of Michael Hanline, who was the longest wrongful incarceration in California history—36 years!

Dave Brubeck was a jazz legend. A pianist and composer, Brubeck's music is known for employing unusual time signatures and superimposing contrasting rhythms, meters, and tonalities. The recipient of numerous awards, honors, and recognitions, he received the Grammy Lifetime Achievement Award in 1996.

Walter Brueggemann is a Protestant theologian and considered one of the most influential Old Testament scholars of the past several decades.

Daniel Callahan is a philosopher specializing in biomedical issues. In 1969 he co-founded the first bioethics research center in the world—the Hastings Center.

Arthur Caplan is the Drs. William F. and Virginia Connolly Mitty Professor and head of the Division of Bioethics at New York University Langone Medical Center in New York City.

Sr. Joan Chittister, O.S.B., is a Benedictine nun, author, and speaker. The co-chair of Global Peace Initiative of Women, a UN-sponsored organization of women peacemakers, she has authored more than 50 books. Her most recent is *A Passion for Life.*

George Church, Ph.D., is molecular geneticist. A professor of Genetics at Harvard Medical School and a professor of Health Sciences and Technology at Harvard and the Massachusetts Institute of Technology (MIT), he is also a faculty member at the Wyss Institute for Biologically Inspired Engineering at Harvard University. Dr. Church is a pioneer in personal genomics and synthetic biology.

Jack Coleman is the former president of Haverford College and former chairman of the Federal Reserve Bank in Philadelphia. The author of *Blue-Collar Journal*, Coleman recounts how during his distinguished career he held odd jobs as a roughneck, dishwasher, ditch digger, trash collector, pigpen cleaner and prison guard.

Jerry Coleman was the second baseman for the New York Yankees from 1949 through 1957 and manager of the San Diego Padres in 1980. He was also a Hall of Fame broadcaster and decorated fighter pilot during World War II and the Korean War.

Marva Collins is a legendary educator and recipient of the National Humanities Medal. In 1975 she founded Westside Preparatory School, a private school for low-income youth in Garfield Park on the west side of Chicago. Many of her students, who were deemed uneducable by the Chicago public school, graduated from Westside Prep and attended prestigious colleges and universities throughout the U.S.

Dalton Conley is a sociologist. A university professor and formerly the dean for the Social Sciences and chair of the Department of Sociology at New York University, Conley is the author of several books, including the memoir *Honky* and a sociological study of class stratification for the general reader entitled *The Pecking Order*.

Richard Cook is a former U.S. federal government analyst who was instrumental in exposing White House cover-ups of the Space Shuttle *Challenger* disaster in 1986.

Lynne Cox is a long-distance swimmer extraordinaire. In 1972 at the age of 15 she swam the English Channel, setting a new world record for both men and women. Since then, she has undertaken many world-class swims. For example, she swam across the Cook Strait, the Straits of Magellan, around the Cape of Good Hope, across Glacier Bay, Alaska, as well as a one-mile swim to Antarctica in 32-degree water.

Albert G. Crenshaw, Ph.D., is an associate professor in the Centre for Musculoskeletal Research in Umeå, Sweden. In 1994 Crenshaw was the first African-American to earn a doctoral degree in the medical sciences in Sweden. His research focuses on muscle physiology with emphasis on mechanisms of muscle pain. Crenshaw has co-authored more than 50 research papers in the fields of ergonomics and in sports and work physiology. He is a current reviewer of submitted manuscripts for 15 journals. In the 1970s he worked in Orthopedic Research at UC San Diego and in late 1980s he worked for NASA's Ames Research Center just outside San Francisco.

Nonie Darwish is an Egyptian-American human rights activist and critic of Islam. She is the founder of Arabs for Israel and the director of Former Muslims United.

William Michael Dillon is a free man. He was released from prison in November 2008 after serving 27 years for a murder he didn't commit. Post-conviction DNA testing verified his innocence. At release, Dillon's 27 years was the longest served by a DNA exoneree in the U.S.

Rev. Thomas Doyle, O.P., is a Catholic priest who exposed clergy sexual abuse of children in the 1980s. He has served tirelessly as an expert witness in trials of alleged sexual abuse in the U.S., Canada, Ireland, Israel, and Great Britain.

Daniel Ellsberg is a longtime peace activist who leaked the *Pentagon Papers,* a secret history of the Vietnam War, to the *New York Times*. Arrested and convicted of 12 felony counts, Ellsberg could have been sentenced to more than 100 years in prison if found guilty. Judge Matthew Byrne declared a mistrial in his case after it was revealed that President Nixon approved a break-in at the office of Ellsberg's psychiatrist.

Greg Evans is a cartoonist and the creator of the syndicated comic strip *Luann*. He received the 2003 National Cartoonists

Society Reuben Award for the strip.

Gayle Lynn Falkenthal is the owner of the Falcon Valley Group, a public relations and strategic communications firm in San Diego. Previously, she was an award-winning broadcast editor and producer with KOGO-AM Radio, KPBS-FM Radio, and KFMB TV.

Kenneth W. Ford is a theoretical physicist, professor, and author. He was the first chair of the Physics Department at the University of California at Irvine, former president of the New Mexico Institute of Mining and Technology, and former executive director and chief executive officer of the American Institute of Physics.

Lois P. Frankel, Ph.D., is the author of *Nice Girls Don't Get the Corner Office* and *Stop Sabotaging Your Career.*

Mary C. Gentile is the author of *Giving Voice to Values: How to Speak Your Mind When You Know What's Right.*

Temple Grandin is a professor of Animal Science at Colorado State University, a best-selling author, an autism activist, and a consultant to the livestock industry on animal behavior.

Annie Griffiths is one of the first women photographers to work for *National Geographic* Magazine, photographing in nearly 150 countries in her career. She has worked on dozens of magazine and book projects for the magazine, including stories on Lawrence of Arabia, Baja California, Galilee, Petra, Sydney, New Zealand, and Jerusalem.

Erin Gruwell is an educator and founder of the Freedom Writers Foundation, a non-profit organization, which has won many prestigious awards, including the Spirit of Anne Frank Award. In 2007 the film *Freedom Writers*, starring Hilary Swank as Erin Gruwell, was released. It depicted Gruwell's efforts to inspire her students to practice tolerance, pursue their education, and live for tomorrow.

Victoria Hale is the founder of the first nonprofit pharmaceutical company, OneWorldHealth, to treat infectious diseases at little or no cost to patients in the developing world. In 2006 the MacArthur Foundation named her a Fellow. Today she is the chief executive officer of Medicines360.

Jim Hall was a legendary jazz guitarist, composer, and arranger. His collaborations with Bill Evans, Paul Desmond, and Ron Carter stand the test of time. Recipient of numerous awards, he was honored in 1997 with New York Jazz Critics Circle Award for Best Jazz Composer/Arranger.

Victor Davis Hanson is the Martin and Illie Anderson Senior Fellow at Stanford University's Hoover Institution. He is also a military historian, columnist, political essayist, and former classics professor specializing in ancient warfare. In 2007 he was awarded the National Humanities Medal.

Joy Harjo is a Muskoke (Creek) poet, musician, performer, and writer. She is the recipient of the Lifetime Achievement Award from the Native Writers' Circle of the Americas, a Native American Music Award (NAMMY) for Best Female Artist, and was recently inducted into her tribe's Hall of Fame.

Lynn Harrell is a world-class cellist. He is the recipient of numerous music awards, including the inaugural Avery Fisher Award (jointly with Murray Perahia) and two Grammys for Best Chamber Music Performance with Vladimir Ashkenazy and Itzhak Perlman.

Frances Hesselbein is the president and chief executive officer of the Frances Hesselbein Leadership Institute and is its founding president. Previously, she served as the chief executive officer for the Girl Scouts of the USA.

Jeremy Hollinger is a healthcare ombudsman mediator at Kaiser Permanente in northern California. Previously, he was a member of the Missionaries of Charity Brothers, founded by

Mother Teresa.

Leroy Hood is a distinguished biologist. He is president and cofounder of the Institute for Systems Biology. The inventions developed under his leadership include the automated DNA sequencer and an automated tool for synthesizing DNA. He has received numerous prestigious awards, including the National Medal of Science, the Lemelson-MIT Prize, and the Kyoto Prize in Advanced Technology.

Rev. George Houser is a Methodist minister and pioneer civil rights leader. He cofounded the Congress of Racial Equality (CORE) with James Farmer and Bernice Fisher. He is also a longtime peace activist and author of *No One Can Stop the Rain*.

Mari-Luci Jaramillo is the first Hispanic-American U.S. Ambassador (Honduras). She is the author of *Madam Ambassador: The Shoemaker's Daughter*.

Robert Kenner is a television and film screenwriter, a television and film director, and a television and film producer. He received a Peabody Award, an Emmy Award, and a Grierson Award for his 2005 film, *Two Days in October,* which recounts two turbulent days in October 1967 surrounding the Vietnam War. In 2008, Kenner produced and directed the documentary film, *Food, Inc.*, a scathing exposé of the U.S. food industry. In 2015 the film *Merchants of Doubt* is scheduled for release by Sony Picture Classics. Another film, *Command and Control,* will come out in 2016.

Gloria Killian is the founder and executive director of the Action Committee for Women in Prison. She served approximately 19 years in prison, wrongly convicted for planning the killing of a Sacramento man. The Ninth Circuit Court of Appeals exonerated Killian in 2002 in a 3-0 decision.

Anne Kelly Knowles is a distinguished geographer

specializing in Historical Geographic Information Systems (HGIS). She is chair of the Geography Department at Middlebury College. In 2012 Knowles was awarded a Smithsonian American Ingenuity Award for historical scholarship. Her latest book, co-authored with Amy Hillier, is *How Maps, Spatial Data, and GIS Are Changing Historical Scholarship.*

Ted Kooser is a Pulitzer Prize-winning poet who served as Poet Laureate to the Library of Congress from 2004 to 2006. Author of 20 books of poetry, he published *Splitting an Order* in 2014.

Peter Korn is the executive director of the Center for Furniture Craftsmanship in Rockport, Maine. He is the author of several books, including *Why We Make Things and Why It Matters: The Education of a Craftsman.* Previously, Korn spent six years as program director at Colorado's Anderson Ranch Arts Center and four years as adjunct associate professor at Drexel University. His award-winning furniture has been exhibited nationally in galleries and museums.

Stephen M. Kosslyn is the director of the Center for Advanced Study in the Behavioral Sciences at Stanford University. A psychologist specializing in cognitive psychology and neuroscience, he has authored more than 300 scientific papers and written or co-authored 15 books.

Eugene Kranz was NASA's flight director for the Gemini and Apollo programs. During Apollo 11's historic mission to the moon, he was the flight director for the Lunar Module's descent to the moon's surface on July 20, 1969. He is a recipient of the Presidential Medal of Freedom, the nation's highest civilian honor.

David Krieger is the founder of the Nuclear Age Peace Foundation and has served as its president since 1982. He has lectured throughout the U.S., Europe and Asia on issues of peace, security, international law, and the abolition of nuclear weapons.

Tom Kundig is a principal/owner of the Seattle-based firm Olson Kundig Architects. He is the recipient of many design awards, including a 2008 National Design Award in Architecture Design from the Smithsonian Cooper-Hewitt and a 2007 Academy Award in Architecture from the American Academy of Arts and Letters.

Robert Langer is an engineer and the David H. Koch Institute Professor at the Massachusetts Institute of Technology, author of more than 1,175 articles, holder of approximately 800 issued and pending patents worldwide, and reputedly the most cited engineer in history.

Mel Leipzig is a painter whose work has been exhibited in numerous solo and group exhibitions. The recipient of many awards for his art, he was a professor of the history of fine arts and painting at Mercer County Community College in New Jersey for 45 years.

Daniel Levitin, Ph.D., is a cognitive psychologist, neuroscientist, and writer. He is the author of two bestselling non-fiction books on music and neuroscience—*This Is Your Brain on Music* and *The World in Six Songs.*

Nancy Lieberman is a basketball Hall of Famer of the Women's National Basketball Association, a two-time Olympian, and a three-time All American. She is also the author of *Playbook for Success* and a motivation speaker.

Debra Liebert is a managing director at Domain Associates, LLC, one of the first venture capital firms to invest exclusively in the life sciences sector.

Alan Lightman is a physicist, author of *Einstein's Dreams,* and professor at the Massachusetts Institute of Technology. In 2011 he received a Sidney Award, named after the renowned philosopher Sidney Hook, for his thought-provoking essay

"The Accidental Universe" in *Harper's Magazine.*

David Lim is a retired Lieutenant from the Port Authority Police Department. On September 11, 2001, he survived the collapse of One North Tower. He is the recipient of numerous awards for heroism, including the Meritorious Service Medal from the Port Authority Police Department.

Patricia Limerick is a professor of History and the faculty director and chair of the Board of the Center of the American West at the University of Colorado at Boulder. Considered one of the leading historians of the American West, she is the author of *The Legacy of Conquest*, a landmark reinterpretation of the American West.

Mario Livio is an astrophysicist at the Space Telescope Science Institute, which is the science operations center for the Hubble Space Telescope and the James Webb Space Telescope. He is the author of popular science books, including *The Golden Ratio* and *Brilliant Blunders.*

Phillip Lopate is a film critic, essayist, fiction writer, poet, and teacher. In 2013 he published *To Show and To Tell: The Craft of Literary Nonfiction.*

Alfred Lubrano is a reporter for the *Philadelphia Inquirer* and the author of *Limbo: Blue-Collar Roots, White-Collar Dreams.* His work has appeared in various national magazines and anthologies. For many years Lubrano was a commentator on National Public Radio.

Robert J. Maurer, Ph.D., is a faculty member with the UCLA School of Medicine. He has developed seminars and lectures on the psychology of success and its essential traits. He is the author of *One Small Step Can Change Your Life: The Kaizen Way.*

John McKnight is co-director of the Asset-Based Community Development Institute and professor emeritus of

Communications Studies, Education and Social Policy
at Northwestern University in Evanston, Illinois.

Larry McReynolds is one of NASCAR's most successful pit
crew chiefs and is a racing analyst on Fox Sports and Turner
Network Television (TNT).

Frank Meeink is a former neo-Nazi skinhead, ex-convict, and
recovering heroin addict. After serving three years in prison,
he left the neo-Nazi movement. With the help of the
Philadelphia Flyers hockey team, he founded Harmony
Through Hockey, an organization that fosters tolerance,
diversity, and mutual understanding through hockey. Today,
Meeink is a hockey coach in Des Moines, Iowa, a noted
speaker and lecturer, and the author of *Autobiography of a
Recovering Skinhead.*

Tom Morris is chairman of the Morris Institute for Human
Values. He is a public philosopher and the author of more than
20 books, including *True Success, If Aristotle Ran General
Motors, Philosophy for Dummies,* and *The Art of Achievement.*

Michelle Mueller is a business advisor and community
volunteer. Previously, she was a vice president with San
Diego Gas & Electric.

Michael Nagler is professor emeritus of Classics and
Comparative Literature at the University of California at
Berkeley, the president of the Metta Center for Nonviolence,
and the author of *The Search for a Nonviolent Future.*

Kristin Neff, Ph.D., is an associate professor of Human
Development and Culture at the University of Texas at Austin
and the author of *Self-Compassion: Stop Beating Yourself Up
and Leave Insecurity Behind.*

Eric Neudel is a producer, director, and editor of numerous
award-winning films for public television, including *Eyes on the
Prize, Life Worth Living, AIDS: Chapter One, LBJ Goes to*

War, Tet 1968, Steps, and *After the Crash.*

Carol North, M.D., holds the Nancy and Ray L. Hunt Chair in Crisis Psychiatry and is a professor in the Departments of Psychiatry and Surgery, Division of Emergency Medicine on Homeland Security, at the University of Texas Southwestern Medical Center in Dallas. A former schizophrenic, she authored *Welcome Silence: My Triumph over Schizophrenia.*

Arnold Palmer is a legendary golfer and sportsman. Considered one of the greatest golfers in the history of the game, he was inducted into the World Golf Hall of Fame 1974 and presented with the PGA Tour Lifetime Achievement Award in 1998.

Christine Peterson is a nanotechnologist and the cofounder of Foresight Institute. She is credited with formulating the term "open source."

Mark Potok is senior fellow at the Southern Poverty Law Center and editor of SPLC's *Intelligence Report.*

Sr. Helen Prejean, C.S.J., is a Roman Catholic nun, a member of the Congregation of St. Joseph, a leading opponent of the death penalty, and the author of *Dead Man Walking* and other books.

Donald A. Redelmeier, M.D., is a researcher at the University of Toronto and an internist at Sunnybrook Hospital in Toronto, Canada's largest trauma center. His research has uncovered intriguing findings, such as the survival of Academy Award-winning actors and actresses and the increase in driving fatalities on Super Bowl Sunday.

Adam G. Riess is an astrophysicist who shared both the 2011 Nobel Prize for Physics "for the discovery of the accelerating expansion of the Universe through observations of distant supernovae" and the 2006 Shaw Award in Astronomy with Saul Perlmutter and Brian P. Schmidt.

Roger Rosenblatt is a journalist, playwright, teacher, and author of *Kayak Morning: Reflections on Life, Grief, and Small Boats*. He was a longtime columnist for *Time* Magazine.

Danny Rubin is a screenwriter, actor, lecturer, and blogger. He wrote the screenplay to the 1993 comedy *Groundhog Day*, for which he received a BAFTA Film Award for Best Screenplay.

Douglas Rushkoff is a media theorist, writer, columnist, lecturer, graphic novelist, and documentarian. He is the first recipient of the Neil Postman Award for Career Achievement in Public Intellectual Activity, presented by the Media Ecology Association.

Erica Ollmann Saphire, Ph.D., is a professor in the Department of Immunology & Microbial Science at the Scripps Research Institute, a director of the Viral Hemorrhagic Fever Immunotherapeutic Consortium, and a member of the Scientific Leadership Board of The Global Virus Network. Dr. Saphire published breakthrough studies in the journals *Science, Nature,* and *Cell,* explaining how Ebola virus infected cells and how antibodies can be harnessed to defeat them. She is the recipient of the Presidential Early Career Award in Science and Technology awarded at the White House in 2009.

Vin Scully is a Major League Baseball Hall of Fame broadcaster, the "voice" of the Los Angeles Dodgers for more than 66 years in 2015, the longest tenure of any broadcaster with a single team in professional sports history.

Mubin Shaikh is a former Islamist extremist turned counterterrorism operative.
He is also a subject matter expert and Ph.D. candidate in the psychology of radicalization and terrorism. Born and raised in Canada, Shaikh became a supporter of the militant jihadi culture at the age of 19. The 9/11 attacks prompted him to travel to Syria and study Arabic and Islamic Studies,

deepening his knowledge of Islam. Eventually, Shaikh relinquished his violent interpretations of Islam and volunteered with the Canadian Security Intelligence Service (CSIS) to fight international and domestic terrorism. Working for CSIS, he infiltrated several radical groups and conducted surveillance on suspects as an undercover operative. He went undercover with and was instrumental in prosecuting Canada's largest domestic terrorism investigation known as the "Toronto 18" case. He is the author of *Undercover Jihadi: Inside the Toronto 18—Al Qaeda Inspired, Homegrown Terrorism in the West.*

Michael Shermer is the publisher of *Skeptic* Magazine, adjunct professor at Claremont Graduate University and Chapman University, and the author of *The Believing Brain*.

Dennis Smith is a former New York City firefighter and bestselling author. He has written 14 books of both fiction and nonfiction. He also founded *Firehouse* Magazine and started the Firehouse Muster and Conference held in Baltimore every year.

Bishop John Shelby Spong is a retired bishop of the Episcopal Church. From 1979 to 2000 he was Bishop of Newark, New Jersey. He is a civil rights activist, theologian, religion commentator, and bestselling author.

Frank Sulloway is a visiting scholar at the Institute of Personality and Social Research on the campus of the University of California at Berkeley, and a visiting professor in the Department of Psychology. He is the author of *Born to Rebel: Birth Order, Family Dynamics, Creative Lives* and *Freud, Biologist of the Mind: Beyond the Psychoanalytic Legend.*

Stuart W. Thorn is the chief executive officer and president of Southwire Company, Inc., the leading manufacturer of wire and cable in the distribution and transmission of electricity in North America.

Eric J. Topol, M.D., is a Professor of Genomics at the Scripps Research Institute, the Chief Academic Officer for Scripps Health, and the Director of the Scripps Translational Science Institute. Voted as the #1 Most Influential Physician Executive in the United States in 2012 in a national poll conducted by *Modern Healthcare*, Dr. Topol works on genomic and wireless digital innovative technologies to reshape the future of medicine. He is a practicing cardiologist at Scripps in La Jolla, California. His most recent book is *The Patient Will See You Now.*

Barbara Van Dahlen is the founder and president of Give an Hour, a non-profit organization that has created a national network of mental health professionals who provide free services to U.S. troops, veterans, their loved ones, and their communities.

Emily Warner is the first female commercial airline pilot and captain. She has won numerous awards and recognitions, including the Amelia Earhart Woman of the Year Award. In 2014 Warner was inducted into the National Aviation Hall of Fame in Dayton, Ohio.

David Watson, Ph.D., is the Andrew J. McKenna Family Professor and Co-Director of the Center for Advanced Measurement of Personality and Psychopathology at Notre Dame University.

Jeffrey Wigand, a former vice president of Research and Development at Brown & Williamson, blew the whistle on Big Tobacco in 1994. He informed the media that the tobacco industry had been lying to the American public about the health risks of tobacco for decades. In 1997 a group of state attorneys general and plaintiffs' attorneys won a record $368 billion settlement from the tobacco industry. Today, Wigand is a smoking-prevention advocate.

Ricardo "Cobe" Williams works as a national trainer for the anti-violence organization Cure Violence and the community director of Joakim Noah's Noah's Arc Foundation. He travels the country to train "violence interrupters," individuals who, like himself, are former gang members and now work to mediate disputes in their communities. Williams' work and his personal journey were chronicled in the award-winning film *The Interrupters*, which premiered at Sundance Film Festival and aired on PBS's *FRONTLINE* in January 2012 as a two-hour special. It was picked as one of the best films of 2011 by *The New Yorker, The Chicago Tribune, Entertainment Weekly*, and *The Los Angeles Times*.

Wendy Wong is chief marketing officer for the Ken Blanchard Companies, where she leads integrated marketing and global branding for the organization and its worldwide affiliates.

Harry Wu is a former political dissident who spent 19 years in China's labor camps, which harbor millions of political prisoners. He is the recipient of many awards for his human rights work, including the Freedom Award, presented by the Hungarian Freedom Fighters' Federation and the Medal of Freedom, presented by the Dutch Resistance Foundation. In 2002 Wu was nominated for the Nobel Peace Prize.

Favorite Quotes

David Agus, M.D.
"The people who succeed in life are the people who are well-rounded."

Monica Ardelt, Ph.D.
"By giving of yourself and what you have, you find fulfillment."

Anthony Atala, M.D.
"...[B]e open to the unimagined possibilities that life offers."

Nicole Boice
"Failure is not negative. It just gives you the information that you need to take another route."

Justin Brooks
"Giving hope to the hopeless and freedom to the wrongfully incarcerated have been my passion, my mission, and my life's work."

Walter Brueggemann
"...[W]e live in a society of achievements and possessions and it turns out we can't live by them."

Dalton Conley
"Don't be afraid of offending somebody."

Lynne Cox
"...[I]f you keep trying, you'll eventually figure out what it is you want to do."

Nonie Darwish
"I never lost the sense of being grateful."

136

Daniel Ellsberg
"...[P]ut out the truth and save countless lives."

Greg Evans
"Find a way to make yourself stand out, even just a little bit."

Kenneth W. Ford
"...[W]ithout a core commitment to integrity life is hollow, happiness is illusory, and civilization is impossible."

Lois P. Frankel
"Leap and the net will appear."

Temple Grandin
"Most people stay in their silos, and it's hard to bust out of silos."

Erin Gruwell
"The more you learn, the more it is a burden...What's important is what you do with that burden."

Victoria Hale
"The ultimate reward is serving others."

Victor Davis Hanson
"...[R]emain unaffected by successes...most are transitory..."

Joy Harjo
"Most...stumble about in strange ambitions to own more or to be famous."

Frances Hesselbein
"Find a way to make a difference, however small."

Jeremy Hollinger
"Live the life you want now, and passionately."

Robert Kenner
"Find people who are doing something in a field that you might

want to go into...and learn from them."

Gloria Killian
"Don't be put off by dealing with people from a different world, especially prisoners and the homeless."

Ted Kooser
"Nearly everyone is doing the best they can."

Peter Korn
"We make our own happiness, yes, but there is scant joy to be found in isolation."

Stephen M. Kosslyn
"...[L]earn how better to select your challenges for the future."

David Krieger
"...[E]ach of us has a responsibility to act for the common good and for generations yet to come..."

Tom Kundig
"...[T]hose moments that changed my life were the moments when I took a risk."

Robert Langer
"...[I]f you are persistent and work hard, there is very little that is truly impossible."

Debbie Liebert
"This is your life, live it well!"

Alan Lightman
"The greatest joy in life comes from helping others."

Mario Livio
"Do follow your dreams, but don't hesitate to ask for advice from the more experienced..."

Daniel Levitin, Ph.D.
"I didn't end up doing what I originally wanted to do, but it was a great ride."

Robert J. Maurer
"...[T]ake very small steps...for large change."

Frank Meeink
"I don't count how many times you fall down. I only count how many times you get back up."

Tom Morris
"The key to successful living is to be open to new ideas and new possibilities along the way."

Michelle Mueller
"This is not a practice life—this is your life!"

Kristin Neff, Ph.D.
"We can learn to be happy...by being compassionate to ourselves when we need it most."

Eric Neudel
"We shouldn't care what other people think of us."

Mark Potok
"...[T]he key to living a good life—curiosity."

Donald A. Redelmeier, M.D.
"Respect all that might come to replace you; if not, they will do so more quickly."

Danny Rubin
"Keep going. You're going to like it."

Douglas Rushkoff
"...[S]top looking for the big answer, the ultimate truth, the moment of awakening. There is none."

Erica Ollmann Saphire, Ph.D.
"Learn to communicate…Understand your audience."

Michael Shermer
"To thine own self be true."

Dennis Smith
"You should feel that where you are today is as good as you could make it."

Frank Sulloway
"With persistence, more things are possible than one might think, but not more than one might dream."

Barbara Van Dahlen
"…[W]e can solve the real issues in our world…if we coordinate efforts and if we collaborate."

David Watson, Ph.D.
"If you do what you—not others—find interesting, your life will be satisfying and fulfilling."

Jeffrey Wigand
"…[M]an derives intrinsic happiness…through virtuous action."

Wendy Wong
"One adventure will lead to another."

Harry Wu
"To understand the preciousness of freedom you need to lose it for a couple of years."

Index of Subjects

risk-taker, 107
risk-taking, 4, 5, 102, 105

S

self-centeredness, 32, 33
self-esteem, 23
selflessness, 38
self-worth, 41
service, 4
sexuality, 11
silo thinking, 66, 137
simplicity, 63
small steps, 92, 139
Socratic method, 67
stewardship, 111
strengths, 14, 19, 64
success, 10, 23, 44, 53, 73, 75, 79, 90,
    92, 98, 129, 137, 148

T

the middle way, 90

U

unhappiness, 74
universe, 24, 25, 69, 74, 114

V

Vaillant, George, 32
values, 15, 24, 95, 105
Vietnam War, 123, 126
volunteering, 32, 46, 130

W

waiting, 80
Wales, 87
war, 40, 45, 52, 122
well-rounded, 8, 136
wisdom, vii, viii, 2, 32, 49, 50, 119
world of ideas, 87

Vince Reardon

APPENDIX

Cut a Path, Leave a Trail Assessment Tool

This assessment tool has been developed from the content in this book and is used in the workshop *Cut a Path, Leave a Trail.*

Your Name: _____

Age: _____   Gender: _____   Ethnicity: _____

For each statement mark how much you agree or disagree with that statement. Use the following scale:

1 = Disagree Strongly
2 = Disagree Somewhat
3 = Disagree a Little
4 = Agree a Little
5 = Agree Somewhat
6 = Agree Strongly

1. I am living my life, not someone else's. 1 2 3 4 5 6

2. I enjoy spending times with others. 1 2 3 4 5 6

3. I like learning new things every day. 1 2 3 4 5 6

4. I get things done no matter how long it takes. 1 2 3 4 5 6

5. I like to gamble. 1 2 3 4 5 6

6. I guard my privacy. 1 2 3 4 5 6

7. I depend on others when making an important decision. 1 2 3 4 5 6

8. I enjoy new experiences. 1 2 3 4 5 6

9. I see opportunity in every difficulty. 1 2 3 4 5 6

10. I am confident of success when I undertake a new project.
    1 2 3 4 5 6

11. I enjoy competing with others. 1 2 3 4 5 6

12. I respect authority figures. 1 2 3 4 5 6

13. I enjoy becoming more competent in a skill. 1 2 3 4 5 6

14. I roll up my sleeves when problems arise. 1 2 3 4 5 6

15. I like to take risks. 1 2 3 4 5 6

16. I always say what I think. 1 2 3 4 5 6

17. I would help a family member who needs a loan. 1 2 3 4 5 6

18. I like solving puzzles. 1 2 3 4 5 6

19. I see things through to the very end. 1 2 3 4 5 6

20. I enjoy talking to strangers. 1 2 3 4 5 6

21. I am fulfilled when I achieve goals others can't accomplish.
    1 2 3 4 5 6

22. I always try to get along with others. 1 2 3 4 5 6

23. I enjoy visiting museums. 1 2 3 4 5 6

24. I easily get distracted when working on a big project. 1 2 3 4 5 6

25. I seek out adventure when I go on vacation. 1 2 3 4 5 6

Assessment Description
There are five subsets of the Finding Your Path Scale (FYP-I):
1) Independent (Be Yourself),
2) Other-Focused (Be for Others),
3) Knowledge-Seeker (Be a Learner),
4) Determined (Be Persistent), and

5) Adventurous (Be a Risk-Taker).

All assertions in the Scale are "I" statements expressed positively. To score, count the numerical value of each response and divide by 5. Hypothetically, one could score a low of 25 and a high of 150. A high score, above 87.5 (midpoint), indicates you are in varying degrees independent, other-focused, a knowledge-seeker, determined, and adventurous, i.e., *a pathfinder.* You know where you are going in your life and how to get there. In contrast, a low score, below 87.5, indicates you are lacking these five key qualities in varying degrees. You lack direction in life and are unaware of resources to help you reach your goals.

Below are the five subsets and their corresponding statements. The numbers in parentheses reflect where the statements appear in the Scale.

Independent
(1) I am living my life, not someone else's.
(6) I guard my privacy.
(11) I enjoy competing with others.
(16) I always say what I think.
(21) I am fulfilled when I achieve goals others can't accomplish.

Other-Focused
(2) I enjoy spending time with others.
(7) I depend on others when making an important decision.
(12) I respect authority figures.
(17) I would help a family member who needs a loan.
(22) I always try to get along with others.

Knowledge-Seeker
(3) I enjoy learning new things every day.
(8) I enjoy new experiences.
(13) I enjoy becoming more competent in a skill.
(18) I like solving puzzles.
(23) I enjoy visiting museums.

Determined

(4) I get things done no matter how long it takes.

(9) I see opportunity in every difficulty.

(14) I roll up my sleeves when problems arise.

(19) I see things through to the very end.

(24) I easily get distracted when working on a big project.

Adventurous

(5) I like to gamble.

(10) I am confident of success when I undertake a new project.

(15) I like to take risks.

(20) I enjoy talking to strangers.

(25) I seek out adventure when I go on vacation.

About the Author

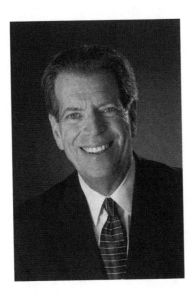

Vince Reardon is an adjunct professor of Communications at The Art Institute of California at San Diego, a noted author, a professional speaker, a mentor, a husband, and a father.

For more than 30 years he has been an award-winning communications professional who has taught more than 10,000 people the art of public speaking.

Vince is an experienced speechwriter and journalist. He has ghostwritten numerous keynotes for CEOs and other senior executives. He also has written numerous bylined and ghostwritten articles in newspapers and magazines, including the *San Diego Union-Tribune*, the *San Diego Business Journal*, *San Diego Magazine*, the *Los Angeles Times*, the *Sacramento Bee*, and the *Arizona-Republic* in Phoenix. In addition, he was a producer, on-air reporter, and radio personality at KJQY-FM 104 in San Diego.

He is a board member and Secretary of *I Love A Clean San Diego* and a mentor at the Preuss School, a charter school for low-income students whose parents never graduated from college. Vince is a longtime member and Distinguished Toastmaster (DTM) of Toastmasters International and a member of the National Speakers Association.

He has a master's degree in Strategic Communications from National University in San Diego and a bachelor's degree in English from Queen's College (CUNY) in New York.

The Pocket Mentor is his second book.

To retain Vince for a keynote speech or a workshop on finding your path in life or your career, contact him at **vincereardon@yahoo.com**.

Connect with Me

at

www.vincereardon.com

21782148R00095

Made in the USA
San Bernardino, CA
06 June 2015